Missing Pieces

Women in Irish History

1: Since the Famine

IRISH FEMINIST INFORMATION PUBLICATIONS Ltd.
with
WOMEN'S COMMUNITY PRESS

©1983 Irish Feminist Information Publications (IFI).

To guard against possible misrepresentation, if any group or individual wishes to reproduce information either in whole or in part from this book, please contact the authors first through the publisher.

First Published in 1983 by
Irish Feminist Information Publications (IFI) with Women's Community Press, 48 Fleet Street, Dublin 2. (01) 716367.

Typeset in 11pt Press Roman by Co-Op Typesetting.

Printed in Ireland by Mount Salus Press Ltd. on 100 gsm white coated cartridge paper.

ISBN 0 946211 01 9

Contributors/Authors/Designers: Dorothy Bell, June Considine, Maureen Cronin, Liz Harper, Maria Holland, Olive Nugent, Irish Feminist Information Publications (Patricia Kelleher, Tricia Coxon, Roisin Conroy).

We gratefully acknowledge the assistance of: Mrs. Canning, Catherine Boland (O'Brien Press), Ester Boyce, Central Remedial Clinic (CRC), Church of Ireland Theological College, Maureen Clare, Prof. Maureen de Valera, Francis Devine (ILHS), Dominican Convent Sion Hill, G.A. Duncan, Feis Ceoil Office, Flying Colours Graphic Studio, Franciscan Sisters, Gate Theatre, John Gibson (Irish Times Library), Noirin Green (Trade Union Women's Forum), Paula Howard (Gilbert Library), Members of Irish Countrywomen's Association (ICA), Irish Independent, Irish Press, Irish Times, Irish Women Workers' Union (IWWU), Mary Jones, Mary Paul Keane, Ellen Kennedy, Anthony Lennon, Margaret MacCurtain, Eric McGrath, Eamonn MacThomais, Medical Missionaries of Mary (MMM), Jenny Murray (IWWU), National Gallery, National Library, Mrs. O'Duffy, Art O'Laoghaire, Nora and Colm O'Laoghaire, Ide ni Laoghaire, Donal O'Looney (National Library), Mrs. Purcell, Religious Society of Friends Historical Library, St. Ultan's Hospital, Annie Scully, Sinn Fein, Sisters of Charity, Sisters of Mercy, Frank Speirs, Jimmy Sweeney (ITGWU), Trinity College Dublin (TCD) Library Staff, University College Dublin (UCD) Archives and Folklore Departments and Library Staff, Chrissie Ward, Margaret Ward and Geraldine Willis, Abbey Theatre.

Special thanks to Margaret MacCurtain

PREFACE

Missing Pieces is a co-operative reference work listing over one hundred women who have made a contribution to Irish life and culture over the last century. As such it is a work of loving restoration, uncovering a wide sample of women who have had an impact on the course of Irish history. By putting women back into the context of their time the authors have contributed an important dimension to our knowledge of the past, as it flows into the present.

It has been said that every story that makes sense and discloses meaning is contagious in its power. This axiom has been ably demonstrated by the remarkable way that *Missing Pieces* has been written. The six women authors involved in its making undertook it as a project begun and completed on a "Women in Community Publishing Course". Irish Feminist Information Publications designed the programme and was the external training agency commissioned by AnCO to implement the nine month course for unemployed women. Funding was provided jointly by the Equal Opportunities Programme of AnCO and the European Social Fund (ESF) with a subvention from the Council for the Status of Women. The rapidity with which the women came together to share a common objective about the nature of the work and communicate to each other the information and skills, as well as the support and excitement, is one of the many achievements that lie behind *Missing Pieces.*

In six weeks they acquired the skills of research, design, layout, planning and editing, and found they had the makings of a book. The decision to publish their findings was just one more step in finding their own power and as a cohesive group they assembled for printing a work of reference which they wrote in simple, clear language for an age group still school-going but also for the enjoyment of the general reader. In itself their project was innovative and inspiring, a chapter of communal harmony, and as such it presents a model of co-operation. Its greatest significance, however, lies in their discernment and convicttion that in publishing these captivating mini biographies they are giving back to Irish history its left out parts. They do not claim to have completed the process; indeed they intend to continue replacing the missing pieces. However, they have in its first volume given a representative spread of female presence in Irish life. *Missing Pieces* is thus not only a courageous revision of the conventional framework of the Irish past, but for those who participated in its making it became a process of setting the captives of that past not only free, but giving them, themselves, back their power.

Margaret MacCurtain
1 July, 1983.

The invisibility of women in conventional histories is remarkable in the light of information contained in this book. Here are 100 biographies of women in Irish history. They come from all classes, from all parts of the country and from all walks of life. We haven't included any women still alive and we had to confine ourselves to 100 words per woman. This is regrettable as the vast majority of these women merit more detailed study. The period covered is from the famine to the present day.

Ireland in 1850 was a rural based society, ruled by Britain. With the possible exception of Belfast, the Industrial Revolution hardly affected Ireland. The injustice of the time included: subjection of Ireland to British rule; lack of agrarian rights for tenant farmers and farm labourers; lack of educational and cultural opportunities; and the insecurity of the urban labouring classes who were at the mercy of unscrupulous bosses. Women of all classes suffered further discrimination by reason of their sex. The wives and daughters of the rich often received a liberal education and owned property, but this was at the whim of their fathers or husbands and was not a legal right.

It was a time of great political mobility both in Ireland and abroad. The spread of industrialisation brought new ideas of liberty and equality. Between America and Europe there was a diffusion of new political theories. In Ireland, different political factions agitated for land reform, women's suffrage, labour rights and Irish Independence from Britain. On the national question, the unionists wanted to retain the link with Britain, nationalists wanted complete independence from Britain and home rulers wanted limited independence from Britain. At this time too, women such as Anna Wheeler, Anna and Fanny Parnell, Louie Bennett, Constance Markievicz and Eva Gore-Booth crossed class boundaries and joined the more oppressed groups in Irish society.

The role of women in an agricultural community based on tillage had lessened with the change to pasture farming. The famine years were a watershed in Irish history. One million people died of hunger at a time when food was being exported from the country. Over a million more people emigrated. However, the changes brought about by the famine created the need for a rethink of values in Irish life.

An 'educational revolution' for women took place in the second half of the 19th century. Before that, women could take exams in Universities but could not attend classes. Alexandra College (1860), the Dominican St. Mary's University College (1886), and Loretto University College (1893), provided places of study where women could attend lectures before sitting university exams. The Royal University of Ireland (1889) was an examining body. It merged with the National University of Ireland (1909), which also conferred degrees on women. Both institutions broadened access to higher education for women and opened the professions to them. The Presentation Order and the Mercy Order founded by Nano Nagle and Catherine Mc Auley respectively, provided primary education for poorer girls. In the late 19th century an educated body of women emerged, drawn from all sections of the community. This coincided with the movement towards an Irish cultural revival and the struggle for women's suffrage. Artists Sarah Purser and Evie Hone and the writer Kate O'Brien contributed to this revival. The suffrage movement, the national movement, the campaign for agrarian reform and the trade union movement attracted many energetic women. Membership of the various organisations often interlocked.

The Land League, founded in 1879 by Michael Davitt and supported by Parnell, aimed at securing for poor tenant farmers what were known as the Three F's: Fair Rent, Free Sale, and Fixity of Tenure. But opposition to the League's radical demands for reform, from conservative middle class nationalists, led to a split between Parnell and Davitt. The Ladies Land League (1881) founded by Fanny and Anna Parnell when the Land League was suppressed, adopted a more radical approach than the men. Members included the poet Katherine Tynan and the 'Nun of Kenmare' Margaret Anna Cusack. An attempt by the Chief Secretary to ban the League, under laws designed to curb prositution, merely enhanced the women's status as nationalists. Parnell did not approve of his sisters' activities and suppressed the League in 1882. Fanny and Anna never forgave him.

Co-operative ideas advanced by Anna Wheeler earlier in the century were revived in 1894. Horace Plunkett founded the Irish Agricultural Organisations Society (IAOS), a non-political association developing the principle of self sufficiency. Plunkett was a unionist, critical of nationalist and home rulers alike. The women's branch of the co-operative movement formed in 1910 had a stronger nationalist outlook. Called the United Irishwomen by writer Susan Mitchell, a contributor to nationalist publications, it is now the Irish Countrywomen's Association.

The majority of women concerned with agrarian reform also campaigned for women's suffrage. The Irish Women's Suffrage Federation (1911) united the scattered suffrage societies and focussed attention on the poor social and economic position of women. A President of the Federation, Mary Hayden, was one of the first women professors in University College Dublin. A further overlapping came in 1911 with the formation of the Irish Women Workers' (IWWU) by, among others, Helen Chenevix and Louie Bennett. Playing a major role in the Irish Congress of Trade Unions, which had been exclusively dominated by men, it won the right to holidays with pay for *all* workers. The IWWU campaigned vigorously for equality of pay and opportunity for members and, until recently, was the only trade union in Europe exclusive to women.

Many of the suffragettes and trade unionists were involved in the struggle for national independence. Inghinidhe na hEireann (Daughters of Ireland) (1900), a revolutionary women's movement founded by Maude Gonne MacBride, merged with Cumann na mBan (1913), the women's auxiliary of the Irish Volunteers. The impulse of these movements – suffrage, land reform, trade union and national – was towards direct action. Women in Ireland believed in deeds and not words.

The medical profession by the 19th century had largely usurped the traditional role of women as healers. 'Wisewomen', who had once passed on the secrets of healing down the female line from mother to daughter, were sometimes regarded as witches. This kind of superstition caused the death of Bridget Cleary as late as 1894. Nowadays there are very few communities where local women perform the tasks of midwifery and the laying out of the dead. But these strong and supportive women are still remembered and talked about in the annals of local history.

Emigration was a sad fact of life in Ireland after the famine. The majority of young girls and women who emigrated found employment as domestic servants. The sadness of their lives is mirrored in the description of life on the lonely Blasket Islands left to us by Peig Sayers.

This book illustrates the contribution made by women to Irish life since the famine. Our lives have been enriched by their achievements.

MARY AIKENHEAD (1787–1858). Founder of Irish Sisters of Charity; born Cork. Brought up as a Protestant, she became a Catholic soon after her mother's death. The archbishop of Dublin, Daniel Murray, asked her to establish a congregation of the Sisters of Charity in Ireland. After three years training in an English convent, she opened the first convent of the Irish Sisters of Charity in North William Street, Dublin. Although plagued with ill-health, Mary's congregation had ten convents opened before her death. She also opened St. Vincent's Hospital in Dublin, the first in Ireland to be run by nuns.

MOLLY ALLGOOD (1887–1952). Actress; born Dublin. Her stage name was Marie O'Neill and, like her sister Sara Allgood, she joined the Abbey Theatre Company. She acted in John Synge's plays and was famous for her interpretation of his works. In his play *The Playboy of the Western World* she was his inspiration for the tempestuous Pegeen Mike. They were engaged to be married before his death. Her career spanned many years in the Abbey and with the Liverpool Repertory Company. She married twice but her second marriage to actor Arthur Sinclair ended in divorce. Although she had many personal problems in her later life it never affected her tremendous acting ability.

MARY AIKENHEAD

MOLLY ALLGOOD

SARA ALLGOOD (1883–1950). Actress; born Dublin. 'You have an actress there', said Yeats when he first saw Sara Allgood in his play *The King's Threshold.* For many years she continued to prove the truth of those words and dominated the Abbey stage during its early, formative years. She married Gerald Hanson in 1916 but their only child, a daughter, died one hour after birth. Her career, though spanning many illustrious years in Ireland, ended in Hollywood with appearances in film and television. She was hailed as 'The one genuine tragedienne of the English speaking stage'.

SARA ALLGOOD by Sarah Purser (detail)

MARY LAETITIA BELL MARTIN (1815–1850). Writer; born Galway. An heiress with an annual income of £5,000, Mary married Arthur G. Bell who had no money and who adopted her name on marriage. (Her father was Thomas B. Martin, M.P., of Ballynahinch Castle, Galway). During and after the famine she spent large sums of money to provide food and clothing for her tenants. Almost penniless, she went to Belgium where she wrote novels to support herself and her family. There is an account of the terrible effects of the famine in her book *Julia Howard* (1850). On a ship to America, Mary contracted fever after the birth of a premature baby and died, soon after arrival, in a New York hotel.

LOUIE BENNETT

LOUIE BENNETT (1870–1956). Suffragist, trade unionist; born Dublin. She was involved in the Irish Women's Suffrage Federation from 1910 and contributed articles to the *Irish Citizen*, a suffragist magazine. She helped form the Irish Women's Reform League which drew attention to the social and economic plight of women workers. Louie was an executive member of the Irish Women Workers' Union (IWWU) for many years. This involved her in several significant campaigns. One such was the laundry workers' strike in 1935 which established the right of workers to paid holidays. In 1932 she became the first woman president of the Irish Congress of Trade Unions.

HELEN BLACKBURN (1842–1903). Suffragist; born Kerry. Her family moved to London in 1859. There she joined the movement for women's suffrage. Helen was secretary of the National Society for Women's Suffrage (1874–95), and also editor of the *Englishwomen's Review* from 1881 to 1890. Her father's illness forced her to give up her suffrage work but, after his death, she began to write. Helen published *Women's Suffrage: A Record of the Movement in the British Isles* (1902). This remained the standard work on the subject for a long time. She also published several books on the working conditions of women.

ELIZABETH BOWEN (1899–1973). Writer; born Dublin. Most of her childhood was spent in Bowen's Court in Co. Cork. This family home was the inspiration for some of her later novels and short stories. *Encounters*, her first work, was published in 1923. That same year she married Alan Cameron. She once said of her anglo-saxon roots that she was only at home in mid-crossing between Holyhead and Dun Laoghaire. This led her, in 1940, to involve herself in England's war effort. The object of her work was to report on Irish feelings regarding the possible seizure of Treaty Ports in the South and West.

CELIA BOYCE (1888–1974). Midwife; born Wicklow. When she was in her teens she travelled with her father to Africa. She married while living there and, with her husband, travelled extensively before coming back to Ireland and settling in Dublin in 1913. Although she had never trained as a nurse she had an instinctive skill inherited from her grandmother and mother who used to act as untrained midwives in their local community. Celia's reputation for capability and kindness grew and in her time she delivered hundreds of local children in and around the York Street area. She epitomised a spirit of co-operation and friendliness that was the essence of a life style that is fast disappearing.

YORK ST., DUBLIN.

ALBINIA BRODERICK (d. 1948). Nationalist; born Cork. A sister of the Earl of Middleton, she never agreed with the unionist views of her family but could not be independent until her father died. Then forty-seven, Albinia trained as a nurse. She built a hospital in Kerry in atonement for the land her family took from the Irish people. She gaelicised her name to Gobait ni Bruadar and joined Cumann na mBan. She became a Sinn Fein member of Kerry County Council in 1921. In 1933 she was co-founder, with Mary McSwiney and Eileen Tubbert, of Mna na Poblachta because they felt Cumann na mBan had become too socialist. She owned the Sinn Fein paper *Irish Freedom* published from 1926 to 1937.

SOPHIE BRYANT (1850–1922). Scholar, writer; born Dublin. In 1894, Sophie was the first woman to be awarded a D.Sc. in Moral Science. She was, also, consultant commissioner to the Board of Education in 1900. She had a lifelong interest in Irish education and culture. This is reflected in her written publications which include *Educational Ends* (1887), *Celtic Ireland* (1889), *The Genius of the Gael* (1913) and *Liberty, Order and Law Under Native Irish Rule* (1923).

ETHNA CARBERY (1866–1902). Poet, nationalist; born Co. Antrim. She wrote the ballad *Roddy McCorley*. Her poems were published in nationalist papers such as *United Ireland* and *The Nation.* She was co-founder, with Alice Milligan of the paper *Shan Van Vocht* which she edited from 1896 to 1899. A collection of her poems *The Four Winds of Eireann* was published after her death. Ethna had a passionate love for the Irish language and was also prominent in the Irish revival in Belfast. In 1901, shortly before her death, she married the Donegal born writer Seamus Mac Manus.

WINNIE CARNEY (1888–1943). Trade Unionist; born Belfast. She was a member of Belfast Cumann na mBan and secretary of the women's section of the Irish Transport Union in Belfast 1912–1926. She became James Connolly's secretary and was with him in the General Post Office during the 1916 Rising. She smuggled a letter out of Kilmainham jail from one of the leaders, Joseph Mary Plunkett, to Grace Gifford (Plunkett and Gifford married just before his execution). Winnie was imprisoned for her activities and on her release returned to the Union office in Belfast. Campaigning for a workers' republic she was unsuccessful as a Sinn Fein candidate in Belfast in the 1918 election.

WINIFRED CARNEY

HELEN CHENEVIX (d. 1963). Suffragist, trade unionist; born Dublin. She was one of the first women graduates from Trinity College, Dublin. Her activities covered a wide range of social issues; trade unions, women's rights, the Labour Party and nuclear disarmament. In 1911 the Irish Women's Suffrage Federation was formed by Louie Bennett and Helen to link together the various suffrage societies. Together they also re-organised the Irish Women Workers' Union (IWWU). The union also campaigned for equal pay and paid holidays. Helen became the third woman president of the Irish Congress of Trades Unions (ICTU) in 1951.

KATHLEEN CLARKE speaking at a meeting

KATHLEEN CLARKE (1879–1972). Nationalist; born Limerick. Kathleen helped to regroup the nationalist forces after 1916 and was interned by the British for this in 1918. She was a vice-president of Cumann na mBan and in 1921 was elected to the Second Dail. She was an Alderman on Dublin Corporation in 1922, elected to the Dail again in 1927 and a Fianna Fail Senator in the 1930's. Kathleen was the first woman Lord Mayor of Dublin in 1939. She broke with Fianna Fail in 1943 (because of a disagreement over policies). She was the widow of Tom Clarke, a 1916 leader.

BRIDGET CLEARY (c1868–1894). Victim of superstition; born Tipperary. Reputed to be the last 'witch' burned in Europe, she disappeared from her home near Clonmel in March 1894. Her body was later found buried nearby and an inquest found that her death was caused by extensive burns. Her husband Michael Cleary and her father Patrick Boland were among those charged and found guilty of her manslaughter at their trial in Clonmel on 4/5 July 1894. The proceedings were reported in the Irish Times of the day. Michael Cleary was sentenced to twenty years penal servitude. It seems from the evidence given at the trial that the defendants thought that Bridget was bewitched when they killed her.

LILY COMERFORD (c. 1900–1969). Dancing teacher; born Dublin. She trained as a dancer at the Maxwell Brewer Academy of Irish Dancing. She had a great interest in children and was soon running her own dancing classes once a fortnight and charging a penny a lesson. At a time when Irish dancing was virtually unheard of outside Ireland she danced in the Albert Hall and London Palladium on several occasions. For ten years in a row she won the Feis Atha Cliath Shield. During a tour of Germany with her troupe in the mid thirties she was asked to dance before Adolf Hitler. She became a legend in her own time and letters addressed to 'Lily Comerford, Post Office, Dublin', were forwarded to her without delay.

MAIRE COMERFORD (1893–1982). Republican; born Wicklow. She became involved in the anti-recruitment campaign during the First World War. Inspired by the 1916 Rising, she worked for Sinn Fein during the War of Independence. Maire was imprisoned during the Civil War but released after going on a twenty-seven day hunger strike. She collected funds in America for the republican cause. In 1935 she joined the *Irish Press* and worked there for thirty years. Although she cut her ties with the republican movement in 1941 Maire retained her interest in the republican cause until her death. She was active in the Anti-Partition League formed in 1947.

LILY COMERFORD

MAIRE COMERFORD

HELENA CONCANNON (1878–1952). Writer, politician; born Co. Derry. She was prominent in the Gaelic League. Helena was elected to Dail Eireann in 1933 and became a Senator in 1938. She contributed to the nationalist magazines of the day and also wrote religious articles for the *Irish Messenger.* Her many works include *Defenders of the Ford* (1925), *Irish Nuns in Penal Days* (1931), and *Poems* (1953).

NORA CONNOLLY O'BRIEN

NORA CONNOLLY–O'BRIEN (1893–1981). Republican; born Scotland. A lifelong socialist and republican, she organised Cumann na mBan in Belfast. Although she arrived in Dublin too late for the Rising, she visited her father, James Connolly, in prison the night before his execution. She became an active worker for the republican movement both in Ireland and America. She was imprisoned during the Civil War. Nora founded the research department of the Irish Transport and General Workers Union (ITGWU). She left the Labour Party when, she felt, they had abandoned their objective of a workers' republic. A Senator for fifteen years, Nora remained totally opposed to partition and the British presence in Northern Ireland until her death.

MARGARET COUSINS

MAEVE CURTIS

MARGARET COUSINS (1878–1954). Suffragist; born Co. Roscommon. She joined the Irish Women's Franchise League in 1908 and attended the Parliament of Women in 1909 in London as a delegate. She was jailed for throwing stones at the British Prime Minister's home in a suffragette protest. She and her husband, James Cousins, went to India where she became a founder member of the Indian Women's Association in 1917. The first woman magistrate in India, Margaret herself was imprisoned for protesting at emergency leglislation. She wrote many articles on art, philosophy and education for Indian periodicals and published several books. Margaret and James Cousins published a joint biography *We Two Together.*

MAEVE CURTIS (d. 1971). Journalist; born Co. Tyrone. She qualified as a Domestic Science teacher in Belfast. In the 1940's she gave lectures to Irish Countrywomen's Association (ICA) Guilds in the Carlow area. Maeve realised the importance of communications, especially for rural women. She established a communications course at the ICA Adult Education College in Louth. This included reporting, magazine and short story writing and radio/television techniques. For many years 'Women's Page' editor of the *Cork Examiner,* Maeve was also honorary editor of the ICA monthly magazine *The Irish Countrywoman.* She was a lecturer at the first, and subsequent, Adult Education courses in University College Cork. Her interests included EEC affairs, consumer affairs and the Irish educational system.

MARGARET ANNA CUSACK (1829–1899). Feminist; born Dublin. Known as the 'Nun of Kenmare', she became an Anglican nun and then a Catholic in 1858. She joined the Irish Poor Clares in 1860. From her Kenmare convent, under the name of M.F. Cusack, she wrote religious books. She also wrote in support of equal rights and equal pay for women. But when she supported the Land League and the Home Rule Movement she incurred the wrath of the hierarchy. With papal permission, she went to America in 1884 to found a religious order to help poor immigrant Irish girls. She was opposed by the Catholic hierarchy there. She reverted to the Protestant faith and ended her days in Leamington, England.

SINEAD DE VALERA (1878–1975). Writer; born Co. Dublin. She trained as a teacher. A member of the Gaelic League, she taught Irish in classes organised by the League. One of her pupils was Eamon de Valera who later became her husband. When her children were grown up she started to write. Her published works include fairy stories, plays and poems for children. She wrote both in Irish and in English. Except for a life-long interest in the Gaelic League, she took no part in public life although her husband served two terms of office as President of Ireland from 1959 to 1973.

SINEAD DE VALERA

CHARLOTTE DESPARD (1884–1939). Suffragist; born England. Known as 'Mrs. Desperate' by Dublin working class, she devoted her long life to radical causes and the emancipation of women. At the end of the last century she was jailed in England after a suffragette protest. She was active during the Lock-Out of 1913. Although her brother, Lord French, was Lord Lieutenant at the time, she supported the Irish Republican Army (IRA) during the War of Independence. Charlotte opposed the Treaty. She went to live in Belfast where she supported the Communist Party in their efforts to unite Catholic and Protestant workers.

CHARLOTTE DESPARD

ANNE DEVLIN (c1778–1851). Patriot; born Co. Wicklow. Her family were related to Michael Dwyer, the United Irishman, and she grew up on a thirty-acre farm in Wicklow. She kept house for Robert Emmet and, after the failure of the 1803 Rising, she carried messages between his hideout in the Dublin mountains and his friends in Dublin. Arrested and brutally tortured, she refused to give any information. By the time she was released, her family were destitute and their farm gone. She lived the rest of her life in great poverty in the slums of Dublin. Towards the end of her life, she was befriended by a Dr. Madden. He had a monument erected over her grave in Glasnevin cemetery.

BIDDY EARLY (c1799–1874). White Witch; born Co. Clare. She became renowned as a 'wise person' with a gift of healing. Her special gift was the cure for eye disease and she was also able to cure illnesses in people and animals. Her gift enabled her to see into the future. The source of her power was reputed to come from a black bottle. It has been described as 'black', 'green' or 'blue'. In the case of her three husbands who all died from excessive drinking there was little argument over the colour – golden malt bottles, donated to Biddy by her grateful patients. Just before her death she is said to have thrown her bottle in Kilbarron Lake. Today her legend remains as fresh and intriguing as ever.

ANNA MARIE FIELDING (1800–1881). Writer; born Dublin. She grew up in Wexford and moved to London when she was fifteen years old. She became a writer and married Samuel Carter Hall. Her works were published under the name Mrs. S.C. Hall. *Sketches of an Irish Character* was her first work. Other published works include *The Buccaneer* and *The Outlaw*. Her husband was also a writer and they often worked together. Between them they produced over 500 volumes. She was also involved in public affairs and started the first fund to further the work of Florence Nightingale. Her drawing room was used for a benefit and over £45,000 was collected.

GERALDINE FITZGERALD (1897–1967). Librarian; born Dublin. She was educated at Alexandra College and graduated from Trinity with a degree in History and English Literature. This was in the early part of the century when a university degree was still unusual enough to be an object of pride or prejudice. By 1917 she was the first woman to be appointed assistant librarian to the Royal Irish Academy. 1932 saw her breaking another precedent when she became the first woman to be appointed to the library of the Church of Ireland Representative Body. When she finally retired in 1962 at the age of seventy, Trinity College conferred an M.A. degree honoris causa for her long dedication to her work.

LUCY FRANKS

MADELEINE FFRENCH MULLEN

LUCY FRANKS (1878–1964). Rural organiser; born Laois. She revived the flagging fortunes of the Irish Countrywomen's Association (ICA) which had just a handful of branches after the turmoil of the Rising and the Civil War. For sixteen years ICA Honorary Secretary, Lucy became Association President in 1942. In the 1930's she was a founder member of the Associated Countrywomen of the World (ACWW), which now has over eight million members. Lucy Franks had a great interest in handcrafts. She encouraged ICA members to display and sell their craftwork at the Royal Dublin Society shows.

MADELEINE FFRENCH–MULLEN (1880–1944). Socialist, Nationalist; born Malta. She was a socialist and nationalist all her life. She joined Inghinidhe na hEireann (Daughters of Ireland) and wrote the children's section for their paper *Bean na hEireann.* As a member of the Irish Citizen Army, Madeleine supervised the medical post in St. Stephen's Green during the 1916 Rising. In 1919 she and her friend Dr. Kathleen Lynn founded St. Ultan's Infant Hospital in Dublin. For the rest of her life Madeleine devoted her energies to social welfare in Dublin, looking after the needs of the poor. She was also, for many years, a member of Sinn Fein.

ANNIE FUREY (1920–1981). Traveller. Annie was the first travelling woman to be housed in Galway. She had ten children two of whom were handicapped by Down's Syndrome. The family had been camping beside a river near Spiddal. Two of her children drowned in this river. Two days later she was given a house in Rahoon. This led to strong objections from the settled community there. Annie Furey was determined to give her children a better life and braved all opposition from the people of Rahoon. She was a noted singer and entertainer related by marriage to the singing group, the Furey Brothers.

MARY FURLONG (1868–1898). Writer, Nurse; born Dublin. From the age of fourteen she was interested in writing. In the beginning her work was rejected by editors with some unwelcome comments but she was a determined young person and did not allow this to interfere with her plans. Soon her poems and stories were appearing in *The Irish Monthly* and other periodicals. At twenty three she became a nurse in the old hospital of Madame Steevens in Dublin. In 1898 she moved to Roscommon to help nurse typhus patients. While she was involved in this she caught the disease and died far from her home and family.

ANNIE FUREY

MARY GALWAY (b. 19th c). Trade Unionist, born Belfast. In Belfast in 1893 she set up the Textile Operatives Society, the first trade union for women textile workers in Ireland. In 1897, Mary led 8,000 operatives against the Truck Act which required employers to post a list of all rules and regulations. The women were successful and achieved significant changes in the regulations. Her union represented the more skilled workers and did not succeed in organising the lower paid women. The unorganised workers turned to James Connolly's Irish Transport and General Workers Union (ITGWU) which led to bitter clashes between Connolly and Mary Galway. She took a leading part in the Irish Trade Union Congress, (ICTU).

Spinning Mills, Belfast

LOUISE GAVAN DUFFY (1884–1969). Teacher; born France. She was one of the first women to attend University College Dublin and took her B.A. in 1911. As a member of Cumann na mBan she worked in the General Post Office kitchens during the Rising but told Pearse she disapproved of the Rising. Louise taught before 1916 in St. Ita's, the school for girls founded by Pearse. After the Rising she founded Scoil Bhrighde, an Irish-speaking school for girls. She left Cumann na mBan in 1922 because of its rejection of the Treaty and devoted herself to the education of girls. Louise received an honorary doctorate from the National University of Ireland for her pioneering work in education.

LOUISE GAVAN DUFFY

ELIZA GILBERT portrait accompanying a gossip item in the Illustrated London News

SIDNEY GIFFORD CZIRA (1889–1974). Journalist, Nationalist; born Dublin. On leaving school, she became active in the national movement, with her sisters Grace and Muriel. She joined Inghinidhe na hEireann (Daughters of Ireland) and began her career with lively articles to *Sinn Fein* and other nationalist journals. Her pen-name was John Brennan. While working as a journalist and campaigning for Irish independence in America, she married a Hungarian emigre. Although blacklisted by the British authorities, she returned to Ireland before the end of the War of Independence. She worked for many years as a journalist and broadcaster. Her memoirs *The Years Flew By* was published in 1975.

ELIZA GILBERT (1824–1861). Dancer; born Limerick. Most of her life she was known as Lola Montez. Married at fifteen, her marriage soon broke up. She was left to cope on her own. Armed with a sense of humour and a strong instinct for survival she became a ballet dancer and appeared in Paris and Munich. The King of Bavaria was fascinated by her and made her the Countess of Landsfeldt with an estate of £5,000 a year and feudal rights over 2,000 people. Her extravagent nature forced her to flee the country when her estates were confiscated. She wrote some light romantic novels, lectured and settled in Australia and America where she entertained at miner's camps. She died in New York in poverty.

MAURA GILL (b. 20th c.). Sportswoman; born Dublin. She was a keen Gaelic speaker and sportswoman. The Camogie Association was formed in 1904 and Maura joined it in 1919. Until her forties she was a skilled and regular player of the game. Her nationalist interests led to her internment in Kilmainham Jail for a short period. She was a long standing member of Croke Gaelic Club. Maura won many All–Ireland camogie medals and captained the winning Tailteann team in 1932. That same year when the Central Council of the Camogie Association was formed she served as its president. She worked in the Cuala Press, a small printing press run by the Yeats sisters which published Irish material.

Cuchullians. One of the first camogie teams, 1904

MAUD GONNE MACBRIDE

EVA GORE BOOTH

MAUD GONNE MACBRIDE (1866–1953). Suffragette, nationalist; born England. Of Irish descent, Maud came to Ireland when she was sixteen. She became involved in Irish nationalist politics and the women's movement. In 1900 she founded Inghinidhe na hEireann (Daughters of Ireland) in protest against the exclusion of women from national organisations. Inghinidhe merged with Cumann na mBan in 1913. She lived in Paris for some years. In 1918, in Dublin, she was arrested and interned in Holloway jail for six months. Maud opposed the 1921 Treaty. In later life she devoted herself to the cause of prisoners' rights and established the Women's Prisoners' Defence League.

EVA GORE–BOOTH (1870–1926). Poet, trade unionist; born Sligo. She wrote poetry and, between 1904 and 1918, had published some ten volumes of verse. Her best known poem is the *Little Waves of Breffny*. Younger sister of Constance Markievicz, Eva supported the women's suffrage movement. In 1892 she joined her friend Esther Roper in Manchester where they worked to better the conditions of Lancashire mill-girls. Their creation of an organised force of women textile workers, recognised by the trade union movement, revived interest in women's suffrage. To obtain decent standards of living for all women Eva campaigned on behalf of such varied groups as barmaids, flower-sellers and women circus performers.

LADY GREGORY (1852–1932). Writer; born Galway. She married Sir William Gregory in 1881. Widowed in 1892, she met W.B. Yeats in 1898. With him, and others, she founded the Irish National Theatre Society. In 1904 Lady Gregory became a founder member and co-director of the Abbey Theatre. She collaborated with Yeats in translating the plays of Dr. Douglas Hyde from Irish. Her home at Coole Park, Roscommon, was the setting for Yeats' poem *The Wild Swans at Coole.* Lady Gregory was the author of many poems, short stories and plays. She encouraged and helped many writers and actors at the start of their careers.

ROSIE HACKETT (d. 1976). Trade Unionist; born Glasgow. A messenger in Jacob's factory in 1910, Rosie was an early organiser of the Irish Transport and General Workers' Union (ITGWU) and lost her job as a result. She joined the Irish Citizen Army, and was active in the Rising. Rosie helped in the printing of the Proclamation of the Republic, and raised the Republican flag over Liberty Hall on Easter Monday, 1916. She ran a first-aid post in the College of Surgeons, was wounded and imprisoned in Kilmainham Jail. Afterwards she worked in the Union shop beside Liberty Hall, Dublin on Eden Quay until her retirement in 1959.

LADY GREGORY

ROSIE HACKETT

CASSANDRA HAND (d. 1868) Rural Organiser. Little is known of her early life. In 1847, when the effects of the famine meant that there was no work for the poor people of the district, Cassandra set up classes in crochet for the local women. Soon 'Clones Lace' was being exported to Europe and America. Although the people were paid little for their work the few shillings they earned kept them from destitution and the workhouse. The work was often done in groups which helped to foster a community spirit in the area. She was married to the rector of Clones, Co. Monaghan.

ANNA HASLAM

ANNA HASLAM (1829–1922). Suffragist; born Co. Cork. Anna was one of seventeen children. She was secretary of the 'Olive Leaf Circle' which promoted universal peace. She advocated equal pay and equal opportunity of employment. She also campaigned for women's rights to higher education and their participation in government. In 1876 she founded the Dublin Women's Suffrage Association, the first Irish Suffrage Society to campaign for votes for women. In 1918 Anna Haslam, at the age of 89, voted for the first time in a parliamentary election.

MARY HAYDEN

MARY HAYDEN (1862–1942). Scholar; born Dublin. Educated at Alexandra College and the Royal University of Ireland where she took a B.A. in 1885 and an M.A. in 1887, in Modern Languages. Appointed Professor of Modern History in University College, Dublin, when the National University of Ireland was founded, Mary was the first woman to serve on the Senate of the NUI from 1909 to 1924. With George A. Noonan she wrote *A Short History of the Irish People.* (1921). She was a member of the Gaelic League and sat on it's executive. Mary campaigned on behalf of women during the 1930's when women's rights to work and to vote were being strongly attacked in the Dail.

CATHERINE HAYES (1820–1861). Singer; born Limerick. She came from a very humble background. Her singing talent was recognised by Dr. Knox, Bishop of Limerick. He raised funds for her to study music in Dublin with a Signor Sapio in 1839. She then studied in Paris and Milan and scored a notable success in the opera 'Linda di Chamourix' at the La Scala Opera House. On an American tour in 1851 as much as 1,000 dollars was paid for a ticket to one of her concerts in California. Whenever she sang in Ireland she was given an enthusiastic reception.

MARIE ELIZABETH HAYES (1874–1907). Medical Missionary; born Raheny, Dublin. At the age of thirteen she told her parents that when she was older she was going to work in the mission fields. Completing her education with a medical degree she graduated with honours in pathology and surgery. She was resident for six months in the Mater Hospital Dublin which at that time was the only hospital open to women residents. Having obtained a final degree in April 1904 she travelled to Delhi in India and was given sole responsibility for a hospital in Rewari. Tragically after only a few years work, she died after a brief illness.

MAUDIE HEALY (1900–1974). Embalmer; born Dublin. She lived all her life in the city and on her marriage moved to a small flat in York Street. With a large family to look after she worked for Fanagan's undertakers in an effort to make some extra income. Her job was washing and laying out the dead. She also did this work for her neighbours and whenever a local person died, Maudie was always the first to perform the necessary work. She was a colourful and witty personality who was known and respected for her contribution to her community.

MARIE ELIZABETH HAYES

EVIE HONE

EVIE HONE (1894–1955). Artist; born Dublin. She studied art in London and Paris. In 1924, she and Mainie Jellett introduced Cubism to Dublin in a joint exhibition of their paintings. She joined Sarah Purser's glass-works at Tur Gloine (Glass Tower) Dublin, in 1932. Evie, Sarah Purser and Michael Healy were all involved in the revival of the Irish stained glass industry. Evie's better-known works include a window in the chapel of Eton College and a window in the Jesuit Church, Farm Street, London. In Ireland her panel *My Four Green Fields* can be seen at the Dublin office of CIE, in O'Connell Street.

HAZEL M. HORNSBY (1900–1980). Librarian; in 1961 she achieved the distinction of becoming the second woman in the history of Trinity College, Dublin (TCD) to receive the degree Bachelor of Divinity. To achieve this she became a Hebrew scholar but her academic career started forty years earlier in 1921 when TCD awarded her the William Roberts Prizeman in Classics. Her studies continued in Oxford and she taught for a short while in Wales. In 1931 she had returned to TCD and was conferred with a Ph.D. She joined the small staff of TCD Library where she remained until her retirement in 1967.

CORA HUGHES (d. 1940). Socialist; born Co. Mayo. An M.A. graduate of University College Dublin, Cora was also the god-daughter of Eamon de Valera but never shared his political views. She was a socialist and a writer and became a member of the Republican Congress in 1934. Cora devoted much of her energies to helping those being evicted from their homes for not paying rent. In 1934 she received a jail sentence of one month hard labour for that work. Cora Hughes died in 1940 of tuberculosis she had contracted while working in the Dublin slums.

ELEANOR HULL (1860–1935). Historian; born England. She was educated in Dublin then went to live in London where she joined the London branch of the Gaelic League. Eleanor was also a member of the London Irish Literary Society. Because of her interest in old Irish she founded the Irish Texts Society in 1899. Eleanor acted as Honorary Secretary of the Society for over thirty years. Her published works include *Cuchulain Saga* (1908), *A text book of Irish Literature* (2 vols, 1906–08), *Poem Book of the Gael* (1912), and *Folklore of the British Isles* (1928).

BAY JELLETT

BAY JELLETT (1902–1983). Musician; born Dublin. She studied music in Dublin, Paris and Manchester. Bay led an orchestral trio at the Gate Theatre where she was musical director for ten years. She toured with the company in Malta, Egypt, Greece and Bulgaria. She became leader of the Gaiety Theatre Orchestra in 1940 and musical director there from 1948 to 1958. Bay and her orchestra played at the Dublin Horse Show each year. She was president of the Cairn Terrier Association of Ireland as well as an active worker for the Dublin Society for the Prevention of Cruelty to Animals.

ANNE JELLICOE

MAINIE JELLETT (1896–1943). Artist; born Dublin. She studied art in Dublin, London and Paris. Mainie, with her friend Evie Hone, introduced Cubism to Dublin when, in 1924, they held an exhibition of their paintings there. Her talent was recognised by the Irish government when, in 1938, she was asked to design the murals for the Irish Pavilion at the Glasgow Exhibition of that year. In 1943 she was a co-founder of the Irish Exhibition of Living Art. Examples of her abstract paintings may be seen in the Dublin Municipal Gallery of Modern Art in Parnell Square.

ANNE JELLICOE (b. 19th c). Educationalist. All her life she fought for the right of equal educational opportunities for women. In 1866 she gathered a like minded group of people about her and opened Alexandra College at 6 Earlsfort Terrace. Serving as Principal from 1866 to 1880, she worked against the prevailing attitudes of the time. People were willing to accept the idea of a school for women but not a college founded especially for higher education. Just after her death her greatest ambition was realised when the Royal University of Ireland, an examining body offering women the opportunity to obtain degrees, was opened in 1881. Her students were now able to continue on to higher education.

MARIE JOHNSON (1874–1974). Trade Unionist; born Belfast. In 1890 she helped James Connolly form the Irish Workers' Textile Union in Belfast to represent the less skilled and low paid mill-workers. In 1913, Marie was active on behalf of the victims of the Dublin Lock-Out, collecting funds in England, and pleading with employers to take back workers. During the Civil War, she was involved in peace negotiations. Elected to Rathmines Urban Council in 1925, she was the first Labour woman on a Local government body in Ireland. Marie was a prominent member of the Women's International League for Peace and Freedom. Her husband was Tom Johnson (later the leader of the Irish Labour Party).

MOTHER JONES (c. 1839–1930). Trade Unionist; born Cork. She trained as a teacher and later went to Memphis. In 1861 she married but six years later her family life came to a tragic end when her husband and four children died of a plague of yellow fever. She became involved in the labour struggle. Miners were soon calling her Mother Jones and she worked unceasingly to better their working conditions. On one occasion during a strike she held her hand over the muzzle of a gun and prevented guards shooting the strikers. Through her efforts she helped secure the passing of the child labour laws in Pennsylvania. Her life was one long struggle against oppression and it spanned one hundred years.

MOTHER JONES

ROSE KAVANAGH (1860-1891). Journalist; born Co. Tyrone. She was determined to make a career for herself as an art student. To do so she moved to Dublin where she turned her talents to writing. She became head of the children's department in the Dublin Weekly Freeman. There, under the name Uncle Remus, she wrote children's stories and became a household name. She was a prolific writer of short stories and poetry. Sadly her promising career was cut short when on a visit home she caught cold and never recovered.

TERESA KEARNEY (1875–1957). Missionary; born Co. Wexford. She entered a convent and in 1898 took her final vows and the name Mother Kevin. Four years later she went to Uganda on mission work. Appalled by the lack of health facilities, and the vast numbers of children dying from malnutrition, she set up her first dispensary. A school for African midwives followed. 1923 saw the formation of the Congregation of the Little Sisters of St. Francis. Schools ranging from primary teaching to teacher training and domestic science colleges were opened by Mother Kevin. To combat the isolation of those suffering from leprosy she founded villages where they could live together. She was known to the old tribesmen as 'a flame in the bush'.

LINDA KEARNS (b. 20th c.). Nationalist. As a nurse during the 1916 Rising she tried to establish a Red Cross post. Active in the nationalist movement, in 1920 she was sentenced to ten years for driving a car full of arms. She escaped from Mountjoy jail in 1921. During the Civil War Linda remained in the Hammam Hotel with Cathal Brugha after it had been evacuated. She accompanied the dying Brugha to hospital. Although a member of Fianna Fail, in 1935 and 1936 she opposed the new laws which affected women's right to go out to work. The International Red Cross awarded her the Florence Nightingale Medal, on her deathbed, for exceptional service.

EVA MARY KELLY (1826–1910). Poet; born Co. Galway. Under the pen name Eva she contributed poetry to *The Nation*. It was strongly rebellious in content and she became known as 'Eva of the Nation'. She became engaged to a young medical student, Kevin O'Doherty. He was arrested for his nationalistic activities in 1848 and promised a pardon if he would plead guilty. 'Be a man and face the worst', she said. 'I'll wait for you no matter how long your sentence may be. ' It was ten years transportation. She continued her career and when, ten years later, he landed at Dun Laoghaire they were married the following day. Eva's best known poems include *The People's Chief* and *Murmurs of Love.*

DELIA LARKIN

DELIA LARKIN (1878–1949). Trade Unionist; born Liverpool. A good public speaker and organiser she was a founder member and first secretary of the Irish Women Workers' Union in 1911. Delia toured England in 1913 organising support for the victims of the Dublin Lock-Out. Always interested in Irish culture, she founded the Irish Workers Choir in 1912, ran dance classes in Liberty Hall, and toured England and Ireland with her Irish Workers' Dramatic Company. Internal feuding in the Irish Transport and General Workers Union (ITGWU) caused her to resign in protest, and she spent the next few years raising funds and organising support for her brother, Jim Larkin, imprisoned in America.

BRIDGET LAWLOR

ANITA LETT

BRIDGET LAWLOR (1881–1969). Entrepreneur; born Co. Kildare. Starting with a small tea-room in Naas, Co. Kildare, Bridget Lawlor created a huge catering empire which supplied the needs of millions at numerous social events. For more than half a century she undertook big and small contracts, banquets, dinner dances, race meetings and dog shows. In the early twenties she got the catering concession for the Spring Show and the Horse Show at Ballsbridge. When work was scarce women with family commitments and unemployed husbands benefited from the part-time work available at Lawlors. The woman who established a European record for the number of meals served also managed a 300 acre farm and bred many winning racehorses.

ANITA LETT (1872–1940) Rural organiser; born England. In 1910 when she was vice-president of the Wexford Farmers' Association Anita founded the United Irishwomen (later called the Irish Countrywomen's Association), in Bree, Co. Wexford. She became the society's first president. Married to a local farmer and prominent businessman, she saw the need for an organisation devoted to improving the life of women in rural Ireland, especially the less well off. Later, in 1925, she started a weaving industry for girls in Enniscorthy which produced tweed from local wool. Ahead of her time, Anita Lett wanted positive discrimination in favour of women. She suggested, in 1910, that they should be nominated directly to important decision-making bodies without standing for election.

CHRISTINE LONGFORD (1900–1980). Writer; born England. Educated at Somerville College, Oxford, she married Lord Longford in 1925. Christine worked with him at the Gate Theatre, Dublin, where she was managing director from 1961 to 1964. She was a member of the Irish Academy of Letters. She wrote many novels and plays between 1931 and 1958. *Making Conversation* (1931), *Printed Cotton* (1935), and *Sea Change* (1940), are some of her novels. Her plays include *Lord Edward* (1942), *Tankardstown* (1950) and *The Hill of Quirke* (1958). Christine also wrote a dramatic version of Jane Austen's novel *Pride and Prejudice.*

MARY CLARE LYNCH (1906–1971). Rural organiser; born in Co. Meath. Involved in farming all her life, Mary Clare had a great interest in rural life and in adult education. She was a founder member of Meath Federation of the Irish Countrywomen's Association (ICA) and supported An Grianan' (the ICA Adult Education College) when it started in 1954. She was very much involved in all local agricultural shows – Navan, Trim, Oldcastle and Virginia – both as an organiser and as an exhibitor, and won many awards for her produce. One of her favourite pastimes was the craft of rushwork. She cut and sold rushes from the river Boyne every year and, with others, re-created an interest in this craft throughout Co. Meath. She and her husband John bred horses, also, on their farm.

CHRISTINE LONGFORD

MARY CLARE LYNCH

PATRICIA LYNCH (1898–1972). Writer, Suffragist; born Cork. Her family moved to London after her father's death. Active in the Women's Franchise movement, Sylvia Pankhurst asked her to report the 1916 Rising in Ireland for *The Workers Dreadnought*. Her pamphlet *Rebel Ireland* gave an accurate account of the happenings in Ireland and was sold in Europe and America. Her first story was published when she was eleven and her first book, *The Cobblers Apprentice* won the Tailteann Silver Medal for literature in 1932. She published over fifty books. In 1920 she married the writer R M Fox and lived in Dublin until her death.

PATRICIA LYNCH

KATHLEEN LYNN

KATHLEEN LYNN (1874–1955). Doctor; born Co. Mayo. She looked after suffragettes who were jailed and on hunger strike and spoke for them at public meetings. Kathleen was an Irish Citizen Army Captain during the Rising. She tended to the wounded and dying and, as the only officer present, took the surrender of the Dublin Castle forces. A Sinn Fein executive member in 1918, she was elected to the Dail for Dublin North in 1923. She refused to take her seat as she opposed the Treaty. For the rest of her life Kathleen cared for the children who came to St. Ultan's Infant Hospital, Dublin, which she helped to found in 1919.

MARY CATHERINE MCAULEY

DOROTHY MACARDLE (1889–1958). Historian, dramatist; born Dublin. A member of the Dundalk brewing family, she was educated at Alexandra College and later taught there. She was jailed for her activities in the republican movement and went on hunger strike. Dorothy took the republican side in the Civil War. Her book *The Irish Republic* (1939) became a standard history about the establishment of the Irish state. *Children of Europe* (1949) describes her work for refugee children during World War II. Her other writings include plays, short stories and two novels *Uneasy Freehold* and *The Uninvited*, both of which were made into films.

MARY CATHERINE McAULEY (1778–1841). Founder of Sisters of Mercy Order; born Dublin. The foundations for her first convent were laid in Baggot Street. This was to provide education for the young, protection for servants and a home for women willing to devote themselves to the sick and dying. In 1831 the order of the Sisters of Mercy was recognised. She was a pioneer in the field of Irish education. Her new order grew rapidly and today the Sister of Mercy Order is established in many parts of the world.

AMANDA MCKITTRICK ROS (1860–1939). Novelist; born Co. Down. She trained as a teacher but was more interested in a literary career. In 1897 she launched her first novel *Irene Iddesleigh* which was published at her own expense. Her high flown style was received with astonishment and some laughter by the public. But she was utterly serious about her work and two more novels *Delina Delany* and *Donald Dudley* followed. This increased her reputation and at Oxford she became the subject of a cult while a club of her admirers met regularly in London. Her collections of verse *Poems of Puncture* and *Poems of Fomentation* were as eccentric as her earlier works and added to her legend.

MARY MACKEN (b. 19th c). Educated at Loreto University College and the Royal University of Ireland where she took her B.A. in 1898 and M.A. in 1900. After further study in Cambridge, Paris and Berlin, in 1909 Mary became Lecturer in German at University College, Dublin. Shortly after, she was appointed Professor of German, a position she held until her retirement in 1950. In her youth she joined Inghinidhe na hEireann, was secretary of Cumann na nGaedheal in 1903 and, in 1906, a member of the Sinn Fein Executive. She was part founder of the Infant Aid Society in 1911 and joined in various efforts to relieve distress in Germany after the 1939–45 War. She was a strong campaigner for women's rights in Ireland throughout the 1930's.

(l-r) MARY MACKEN, MARY HAYDEN, AGNES O'FARRELLY

MARY MACSWINEY (c.1872–1942). Republican; born London. Brought up in Cork where she trained as a teacher, Mary was a dedicated republican and a member of the Gaelic League. She was imprisoned after the Rising. After her release she founded St. Ita's, a school modelled on Pearse's Irish school, St. Enda's. Following the death of her brother, Terence, on hunger-strike, Mary represented Cork in Dail Eireann. She was totally opposed to the Treaty which she described as 'a betrayal'. Active on the republican side, Mary was imprisoned twice during the Civil War. She supported de Valera until he left Sinn Fein to establish Fianna Fail. To the day she died, Mary refused to recognise the Free State Government.

MARY MACSWINEY

SARAH MAKEM (1900–1983). Folk-singer; born in Keady, Co. Armagh. She was a noted singer with a fine low-pitched voice. Her songs, some of them dating back four centuries or more, were about the ordinary people of Ireland. Sarah had a great love of local history. Many of her songs and ballads were based on events in her native county of Armagh. During the 1950's she sang on a radio programme called 'As I roved out'. This stimulated a new interest in the Ulster heritage of music which is drawn from the Irish, Scottish and English traditions in its history.

CONSTANCE MARKIEVICZ

MARY MARTIN

CONSTANCE MARKIEVICZ (1868–1927). Nationalist; born Sligo. She studied art in Paris where she met her Polish husband, Count Casimir Markievicz. In 1908 she joined Inghinidhe na hEireann (Daughters of Ireland) to work for Irish independence and women's rights. An admirer of Connolly and Larkin, Constance shared their philosophy that the nationalist cause could be advanced by social revolution. She was a Staff Lieutenant in the Irish Citizen Army during the Rising. In 1918 Constance was the first woman elected to the British Parliament but, as a Sinn Fein candidate, refused to take her seat. Twice Minister for Labour in Sinn Fein governments, she opposed the Treaty and was imprisoned during the Civil War.

MARY MARTIN (1892–1975). Missionary; born Dublin. She trained as a nurse in England during the first World War and served in France and in Malta. On a visit to Nigeria, in 1921, she was shocked at the appalling conditions there. In 1937 she founded her congregation, the Medical Missionaries of Mary (MMM). She was professed as a nun in 1938 and a year later her order opened a maternity hospital in Drogheda. In 1966 she was the first woman to receive an honorary fellowship of the Royal College of Surgeons in Ireland. Her order have hospitals throughout Africa, America, Italy and Spain.

VIOLET FLORENCE MARTIN (1862–1915). Writer; born Co. Galway. She was educated at Alexandra College and spent most of her life at Drishane the home of her cousin Edith Somerville. They shared an interest in literature and in 1886 a literary partnership began. They published fourteen titles under the pen name Somerville and Ross. Their works include *The Real Charlotte* and *The Irish R.M.* which was recently adapted as a television series. Violet wrote under the pen name M. Ross. She also published two volumes of autobiographical essays *Some Irish Yesterdays* and *Strayaways* which was published after her death. She was injured while out hunting and was confined to her bed for the rest of her life.

CONSTANTIA MAXWELL (1886–1962). Historian; born Dublin. Educated at Trinity College, Dublin (TCD) and Bedford College London. She became a lecturer at TCD and in 1939 Constantia was the first woman to be appointed to a chair in the College, when she was made Professor of Economic History. Later in 1945, she became Lecky Professor of History. Among the many works she published are: *Irish History from Contemporary Sources* (1923), *Dublin Under the Georges* (1936); *History of Trinity College* (1946) and *The Stranger in Ireland: From the Reign of Elizabeth to the Great Famine*. She retired in 1951 and died at Pembury, Kent.

ALICE MILLIGAN (1865–1953). Writer, nationalist; born Co. Tyrone. She invited the Fenian, John O'Leary, to Belfast for the 1798 Centenary commemoration. Her interest in the Irish language brought her to Dublin to study it. To raise funds for Gaelic League classes in Irish, Alice put on historical plays and pageants all over Ireland. She was co-founder, with Ethna Carbery of the paper *Shan Van Vocht* which advocated Irish independence. Alice also wrote for the nationalist papers *United Ireland* and *Sinn Fein*. She deplored the Treaty and was a founder member of the Ulster Anti-Partition Council. Alice was the author of several plays and also published *A Life of Wolfe Tone*. She received an honorary degree in Literature in 1941.

SUSAN MITCHELL (1866–1926). Journalist, poet; born Sligo. She worked as Assistant Editor of the *Irish Homestead* and the *Irish Statesman* both of which were edited by AE (George Russell). She had a gift for light verse and was a noted wit. In a study published in 1916 she satirised the novelist George Moore. Always interested in the education and advancement of women, it was Susan who named the countrywomen's movement the 'United Irishwomen', (now the Irish Countrywomen's Association). She also served on its early executive committees. Her poetry was published in an anthology, *New Songs*, edited by AE in 1904 and in later collections. She died of cancer in 1926.

HELENA MOLONEY (1884–1967). Actress; born Dublin. She worked with the Abbey Theatre for many years, joined Inghinidhe na hEireann (Daughters of Ireland), edited *Bean na hEireann* a militant nationalist magazine founded by Maud Gonne MacBride. At James Connolly's request Helena became secretary of the Irish Women Workers Union (IWWU) in 1915. A council member of the Irish Citizen Army, she was imprisoned for her part in the attack on Dublin Castle in the 1916 Rising. After the Treaty, she went back to organising for her union, and was later honoured with the Presidency of the Irish Congress of Trades Unions (ICTU).

HELENA MOLONEY

RIA MOONEY

RUBY MORIARITY

RIA MOONEY (1904–1973). Actress and Producer; born Dublin. An early acting career began when she was six years old. At sixteen she was singing with the Rathmines and Rathgar Musical Society. She was invited to join the Abbey Theatre Company in 1924. A tour of England and the United States followed and, to gain more experience, she remained in New York for some years as assistant director with the Civic Repertory Theatre. Returning to Dublin she became director of the Gaiety School of Acting. Later she returned to the Abbey and was its first woman producer. She held this position for fifteen years.

RUBY MORIARITY (d. 20th c.). Harpist; born Kerry. From her earliest years she was interested in music. Her father was a musician and played the cello in a band. He taught her to play the harp and after her marriage she became a familiar sight in Dublin's Wicklow Street. It was her stage and her audience; shoppers and workers alike, enjoyed her music. A small dog used to accompany her and sleep on a cushion at her feet. Her husband, a circus strong man, used to carry the harp to and from each venue. She had a wide repertoire of tunes and would play special requests for people. Ruby is fondly remembered, to this day, by the people of Dublin.

LILY O'BRENNAN (1878–1948). Nationalist and Writer; born Dublin. Educated at Dominican Convent, Eccles Street, Lily fought in the Rising. Afterwards, with her sister and other relatives of the 1916 leaders, she organised on behalf of the prisoners and their dependents. In 1917 she became an executive member of Cumann na mBan and during the War of Independence she worked for the Republican Paper *The Irish Bulletin.* Lily was one of the secretaries who accompanied the delegates to London when the Treaty was agreed upon but she took an anti-Treaty line. She was jailed during the Civil War because of her views. In later years she devoted her time to writing.

CHARLOTTE O'BRIEN (1845–1909). Poet; She was concerned with many social problems and wrote pamphlets recommending reforms. Her observations on emigrant conditions were reprinted in the *Pall Mall Gazette* on 6 May 1881. The result was a Board of Trade investigation into the White Star Shipping Line and stricter government control of emigrant ships. She was an active supporter of the Land League and contributed to nationist papers such as *The Nation* and *United Ireland.* Her published work includes *Light and Shade* (1878), *Drama and Lyrics* (1880), and *Lyrics* (1886).

KATE O'BRIEN

KATE O'BRIEN (1897–1974). Writer; born Limerick. She was a journalist in London and then a teacher. After some time in Spain as a governess, she returned to London and married Gustav Renier in 1924. Her writing career began in 1926 with the play *Distinguished Villas*. Her first novel *Without My Cloak* plublished in 1931 received the Hawthornden Prize. Other novels included *The Ante-Room* in 1934 and *Mary Lavelle* in 1936. *The Land of Spices* published in 1941 was banned in Ireland. In 1947 she was elected a member of the Irish Academy of Letters. She lived in Co. Galway from 1950 to 1961 when she returned to England where she lived until her death.

KATIE O'CONNOR (centre)

KATIE O'CONNOR (1900–1983). Printer, Trade Unionist; born Dublin. She was active in the Irish Women Workers Union (IWWU). Katie was involved in the 1916 Rising at the age of sixteen and was a messenger between the different garrisons. She was imprisoned in Kilmainham Jail. Katie worked in the Fodhla Printing Company since its foundation in the mid-twenties and was a forewoman in the bindery section.

KATHLEEN O'ROURKE

AGNES O'FARRELLY, (b. 19th c.). Lecturer, Writer; She was educated at St. Mary's Dominican Academy and awarded her M.A. Degree in 1900. With a strong interest in the revival of the Irish language she made many visits to the Aran Islands to perfect her knowledge. Years of service on the executive of the Gaelic League and Camogie Association helped the growth of those movements. She was first principal and president of the Irish College at Cloghaneely. Despite a busy career she became honorary general secretary of the various Celtic Congresses and maintained close links with other Celtic Peoples. In 1932 she was appointed to the Seanad and the Professorship of Modern Irish Poetry.

KATHLEEN O'ROURKE (1906–1980); P.E. Instructor, born Cavan. She grew up in Ballyconnell, Co. Cavan, where her father was the dispensary doctor. In 1933, after three year's training in Liverpool, she qualified as an Instructor in Physical Education. She joined the League of Health and Beauty in Dublin in 1934. The League ran classes in physical education for women and school-children. At that time there were no facilities for remedial care of child polio victims. Kathleen started to treat these, and other sick children, in her own flat at Sandymount. Her compassion and concern opened people's eyes to the plight of the handicapped. This led, in 1940, to the establishment of the Central Remedial Clinic (C.R.C.).

ELIZABETH OWENS BLACKBURNE (1848–1892). Writer; born Slane, Co. Meath. During her young years she lost her sight and was blind for many years. Eventually Sir William Wilde (father of Oscar Wilde) operated on her and restored her sight. By 1873 she had decided to make a literary career for herself and against a lot of opposition, finally succeeded. *The Glen of Silver Birches, Shadows in the Sunlight, A Woman Scorned* were among her works while the well known reference work *Illustrious Irish Women* was also written by her.

ANNA CATHERINE PARNELL (1852–1911). Nationalist; born Co. Wicklow. The founding of the Land League in 1879 led to an increase in agrarian trouble, and Gladstone reacted by arresting the principal leaders, including Charles Stuart Parnell. A supporter of her brothers activities, Anna Parnell founded the Ladies Land League, to take over the direction of the original League. Branches were organised throughout the country and £60,000 was distributed in relief. When the Ladies Land League sought funds to discharge debts, Charles disbanded it on his release from prison. Anna never forgave him, and this episode eventually turned her towards Sinn Fein.

FANNY PARNELL (1849–1882). Poet, nationalist; born Co. Wicklow. She was involved with the powerful Fenian Society. Fanny's poems appeared in the Irish Republican Brotherhood paper *The Irish People.* She went to America in 1874 and founded a branch of the Ladies Land League which she had established in Ireland with her sister Anna. She published poems in support of the League in nationalist magazines such as *The Nation, The Irishman, United Ireland,* and the American *Boston Pilot.* As her health broke down, her writings became more morbid. This is reflected in her poem *After Death,* which was written shortly before her own death, at the age of 28.

ANNIE W. PATTERSON (1869–1934). Musician, Writer; born Co. Armagh. She was educated in Dublin at Alexandra College and the Royal Irish Academy of Music. From 1892 to 1926 she was an examiner in music and worked in music colleges throughout the country. From 1924 she was a lecturer in Irish music at University College Dublin. Despite an extremely busy life she became renowned as a church organist in Dublin, conducted the Dublin Choral Union and was a founder member of the Feis-Ceoil. Her written works include *The Story of Oratorio* and *Chats with Music Lovers.*

SARAH PURSER (1849–1943). Artist; born Dublin. When the family business failed, she studied art in Dublin and Paris and made her living as a portrait painter. In 1903 she founded a stained-glass workshop in Dublin and became a driving force in the revival of the industry in Ireland. In 1924 she founded the Friends of the National Collections in Ireland. Sarah also helped in the establishment of the Dublin Municipal Gallery of Modern Art. A noted wit, she is credited with the comment 'Some men kiss and tell, but George Moore tells and doesn't kiss'. About her commissioned work as a portrait painter she said she had 'gone through the aristocracy like measles'.

ANNIE W PATTERSON

EDEL QUINN (1907–1944). Missionary; born Co. Cork. She was a deeply religious girl and hoped to join the Poor Clare Order. A serious illness shattered her plans. Suffering from advanced tuberculosis she entered a sanitorium where she spent the next eighteen months. She had been deeply involved in the Legion of Mary and, on 24th October 1936, she left Ireland for Nairobi to work as a lay missionary. Her health was never strong yet the next thirteen years of her life were dedicated to the setting up of Legion of Mary Preasidia in Nairobi, Kenya, Uganda, Mauritius and Nyasaland.

EDEL QUINN

LOLA RIDGE (1883–1941). Journalist; born Dublin. She spent her childhood and early life in Australia and New Zealand. In 1907 she went to live in America. She supported herself by writing for popular magazines. For a time she was editor of Alfred Kreymbourg's two liberal magazines *Others* and *Broom*. Lola, with other liberals, went to Boston in 1927 to protest at the execution of the anarchists Sacco and Vanzetti. She was awarded a Guggenheim Fellowship in 1935.

HANNA SHEEHY SKEFFINGTON

PEIG SAYERS (1873–1958). Islander, Story teller; born Co. Kerry. She spent several years 'in service' After an arranged marriage with Padraig O'Giuthin she moved to the Great Blasket Island. She had ten children, of whom six survived. Her children emigrated, her husband died, and Peig was left alone with a blind brother-in-law. She was a well known story teller among the islanders and she recited 375 stories, and forty folksongs to the Irish Folklore Commission. She dictated her autobiography *Peig* to her son Michael, and it was published in 1936. A further instalment appeared in 1970. After 1953, the people of the island were resettled on the mainland, and Peig died in hospital there.

HANNA SHEEHY SKEFFINGTON (1877–1946). Suffragist; born Dublin. She was a graduate of the Royal University of Ireland. She and her husband Francis Skeffington founded the Irish Women's Franchise League in 1908 and published the *Irish Citizen.* She was active in the 1916 Rising, running messages between the different garrisons and getting medical aid for the wounded. After her husband was brutally murdered by the crown forces, she succeeded in getting an official enquiry into his death. She visited America twice seeking support for the republican cause. A Sinn Fein executive member, she served as a judge of the Dail Court and opposed the Treaty. Hanna was a founder member of the Women's Social and Progressive League.

BETTY SINCLAIR (1908–1981). Trade Unionist. born Belfast. She grew up in a Belfast tenement and after a scanty education, went to work in a factory. Inspired by James Connolly's writings, she joined the Revolutionary Worker's Group (which later became the Communist Party of Ireland), and played a prominent role in Belfast's labour movement. In 1947, she became secretary of the Belfast and District Trades Union Council. During her thirty years work for the Council, she also ran a free citizens' advice bureau, providing information on social services, housing and welfare rights. In the late sixties, she helped to set up the Northern Ireland Civil Rights Association (NICRA).

MARGARET SKINNIDER (c. 1893–1971) Nationalist, Teacher; born Glasgow of Irish parentage. She was a member of Glasgow's Cumman-na-Mban and an expert markswoman. In 1913 she came to Ireland on a visit and brought across a supply of explosives. Journeying across by boat she slept on a pillow filled with detonators and the wires were wrapped under her coat. She became a spy for Constance Markievicz and involved herself in many successful raids to obtain explosives for the 1916 rising. During this period she was a dispatch rider between Stephen's Green and the GPO. When the takeover of the College of Surgeons took place, she climbed up on the rafters and fired at British soldiers on the Shelbourne roof. This, she felt, was her duty as the new constitution incorporated equal suffrage. She was shot three times but survived and in later years was an active member of the Primary School Teacher's Association.

BETTY SINCLAIR

MARGARET SKINNIDER

ANNIE M.P. SMITHSON (1873–1948). Writer and Nurse; born Dublin. She was educated in Dublin and Liverpool. She became a nurse and practised as a district nurse in many parts of Ireland. One of the first members of the Irish Nurse's Organization (INO) she served on its committee from 1929–1942. She also edited their magazine. During the Civil War she took the republican side and attended the wounded at the siege in Moran's Hotel. *Her Irish Heritage*, a first novel was published in 1917. It was a best seller and the start of a literary career. She was an extremely popular writer and wrote many romantic novels. *Myself and Others* was her autobiography.

ANNIE SMITHSON

EDITH SOMERVILLE

EDITH ANNA SOMERVILLE (1858–1949). Writer; born Corfu. Her family returned to their home in Drishane Co. Cork when she was eleven. She was educated at Alexandra College and studied art in Paris. In later years she illustrated many of the books she wrote jointly with her cousin Violet Florence Martin. She was a keen huntswoman and on becoming Master of the Fox Hounds led the hunt until 1919. She was a founder member of the Academy of Letters which, in 1932, was founded by William Yeats and George Bernard Shaw to promote bi-lingual creative literature in Ireland. Edith Somerville maintained that their partnership continued on a spiritual level after Violet Martin died and claimed that she was co-author of a biography of their grandfather *Incorruptible Irishmen.*

DOROTHY STOPFORD PRICE

ALICE STOPFORD GREEN (1847–1929). Historian; born Co. Meath. In 1874 her family moved to London where she later married an historian, John Richard Green. After his death she completed and published the books she had helped him to write. Her study of Irish history led her to support Home Rule for Ireland. Alice formed a committee in London to raise funds for the Irish Volunteers. Although critical of the Rising, after 1916 she moved back to Ireland. In 1918 she wrote *Ourselves Alone in Ulster*, a pamphlet attacking the policies of Edward Carson. Alice was a strong supporter of the Treaty and was nominated to the first Irish Senate in 1922.

DOROTHY STOPFORD PRICE (1890–1954). Doctor; born Dublin. She qualified in medicine at Trinity College Dublin. Her book *Tuberculosis in Childhood* was published in 1942. Her earlier research in this area involved the BCG vaccination of thirty-five children in 1936 at St. Ultan's Hospital for Infants, Dublin. This pioneering work paved the way for the Dublin Corporation BCG scheme in 1948. Dorothy's efforts to establish an Anti-Tuberculosis League were opposed by Dr. John Charles McQuaid, then Archbishop of Dublin. She later received recognition for her efforts in the fight against tuberculosis when she was asked to chair the National BCG Committee in 1949.

KATHERINE TYNAN (1861–1931). Writer; born Dublin. Influenced by the Fenian leader, John O'Leary, she was a supporter of the Land League. Katherine published many books of verse including; *Shamrock* (1887), and *Collected Poems* (1930). One of her best-known poems *All in the April Evening* was set to music. She wrote over one hundred novels. Her autobiography mentions many of the well-known literary figures of her time. She was closely associated in the national literary revival in Ireland with people like W.B. Yeats and AE (George Russell). Her daughter is the novelist Pamela Hinkson.

ROISIN WALSH (d. 1945). Librarian; She originally started work as a children's librarian in Rathmines then helped organise Galway Library service. On being appointed chief librarian for Dublin city she undertook the difficult task of unifying Dublin's independent district libraries. In 1930 the Corporation allocated a sum of £20,000 for the building of libraries in the suburbs. She was responsible for the opening of libraries in Phibsboro, Drumcondra, Inchicore, Ringsend, Marino, and Templeogue. She had a difficult and challenging job and an obituary written by a colleague summed up the dedication she brought to her work. 'The phenomenal growth of the service under her direction is, in itself, an indication of the success she achieved.'

ANNA WHEELER (b. 1785). Social reformer; writer; She was prominent in the co-operative movement started by social reformer William Thompson in Cork. At the age of 15 she had the misfortune to marry Francis Massey Wheeler, the son of a Limerick landlord. The marriage was a disaster. Anna fled to Britain with her six daughters. Her experience of marriage is reflected in the passages on the subject of men in the book *Appeal of One Half of the Human Race, Women. . .* , which she wrote with Thompson. She was bitterly opposed to the unbreakable bonds and unequal moral standards imposed upon married women at that time. Anna once wrote "Shall men be free and a woman a slave. . . . never say I".

JENNIE WYSE POWER (d. 1967). Nationalist; The widow of a Fenian, she became involved in the Ladies Land League of 1881–2. Jennie was one of the first vice-presidents of Inghinidhe na hEireann (Daughters of Ireland) and vice-president of Sinn Fein in 1911. After the Rising and during the War of Independence she was on the executive of Cumann na mBan but resigned because of its rejection of the Treaty. Her restaurant in Henry Street had been a meeting-place for nationalists. She was a Free State Senator until 1936. Jenny opposed the Conditions of Employment Bill of 1935 because it restricted the employment opportunities of women.

To the Memory

OF THE

Unknown Women

FAITHFUL AND UNNUMBERED

WHO

IN EVERY AGE OF IRELAND'S AGE LONG STRUGGLE

HAVE DIED OF HUNGER AND HARDSHIP

BUT

ERE THEY WERE GATHERED

INTO THEIR FORGOTTEN GRAVES

PASSED ON

STILL LIVING

The Unconquerable Spirit

OF THE

Irish Race

Dedication in Helena Concannon's "Daughters of Banba", Gill and Son, 1922

BIBLIOGRAPHY

BERE, Thelka J. (Chair). Commission on the Status of Women: Report to Minister for Finance. Dublin: Stationery Office, 1972.

BLACKBURN, Helen (ed). Englishwomen's Review (National Library).

BLACKBURN, Helen (ed). Englishwomen's Journal (National Library).

BOLGER, Patrick. The Irish Cooperative Movement: It's History and Development. Dublin: IPA, 1977.

BOYLAN, Henry. A Dictionary of Irish Biography. Dublin: Gill and Macmillan, 1979 (1978).

BOYLE, Emily. The Linen Strike of 1872. Dublin: Saothar 2 (Journal of Irish Labour History Society) 1976.

CLAFFEY, Una. The Role of Women in the Early Irish Labour Movement (unpublished paper) Dublin, 1975.

COLLIS, Maurice. Sommerville and Ross: A Biography. London: Faber, 1968.

CONLON, Evelyn. The Historical Point of Continuity and Discontinuity in the Women's Movement in Ireland. (unpublished paper). Maynooth College; 1978.

CONLIN, Lil. Cumann na mBan and the Women of Ireland. Kilkenny People Press, 1969.

CONNOLLY, James. The Re-conquest of Ireland (Chapter on 'Women'). Dublin: New Books, 1972 (1915).

COUSSINS, J.M. and M.E. We Two Together. Madras, 1950.

COXHEAD, Elizabeth. Daughters of Erin. Bucks: Colin Smyth, 1979 (1965).

CURRICULUM DEVELOPMENT UNIT. Divided City: Portrait of Dublin 1913. Dublin O'Brien Press, 1978.

DALY, Mary E. Women in the Irish Workforce from Pre-industrial to Modern Times. Dublin: Saothar 7 (Journal of Irish Labour History Society), 1978.

DEVINE, Francis. Women in the Irish Movement: A note. Dublin: Oibre 2 (Journal of the Irish Labour History Society) 1975.

FEENEY, Mary. Alexandra College and the Higher Education of Women 1886 (Thesis). Dublin: 1977.

FOX, R.M. The History of the Irish Citizen Army. Dublin: James Duffy, 1943.

FOX, R.M. Louie Bennet: Her Life and Times. Dublin: Talbot Press, 1957.

FOX, R.M. Rebel Irishwomen. Dublin: Talbot Press, 1967 (1935).

FFRENCH EAGER, Irene. Margaret Anna Cusack A Biography: One Woman's Campaign for Women's Rights. Dublin: Arlen House, 1979 (1970).

GALLAGHER, S.F. (ed) Women in Irish Legend, Life and Literature. Bucks: Colin Smyth, 1983.

GLENDINNING, Victoria. Portrait of a Writer: Biography of Elizabeth Bowen. London: Weidenfield and Nicolson, 1977.

HICKEY, D.J. and J.E. Doherty. A Dictionary of Irish History since 1800. Dublin: Gill and Macmillan, 1980.

IRISH FEMINIST INFORMATION PUBLICATIONS (IFI). Irish Women's Diary and Guide Book 1982 and 1983. Dublin: IFI, 1982, 1983.

JACKSON, T.A. Ireland Her Own: An Outline History of the Irish Struggle of National Freedom and Independence. London: Cobbett Press, 1946.

KEARNS, Linda. In Times of Peril. Dublin: Talbot Press, 1922.

LEWENHAK, Sheila. Women and Trade Unions: An Outline of Women in the British Trade Union Movement. London: E. Benn, 1977.

LITTLE, William. Illustrated London News. London William Little, 1847.

LYONS, J.B. Brief Lives of Irish Doctors. Dublin: Blackwater Press, 1978.

MCCARTHY, Charles. Trade Unions in Ireland 1894–1960. Dublin: IPA, 1977.

MACCURTAIN, Margaret and Donncha O Corrain (eds). Women in Irish Society: The Historical Dimension. Dublin: Arlen House, 1978.

MCDOWELL, P.B. Alice Stopford Green. Dublin: Allen Figgis, 1969.

MCHUGH, Roger and Maurice Harmon. Short History of Anglo Irish Literature. USA: Barnes and Noble, 1982.

MACKENZIE, Midge. Shoulder to Shoulder: A Documentary. London: Allen Lane, 1975.

MARRECO, A. Rebel Countess: The Life and Times of Constance Markievicz. London: 1967.

MILL, John Stuart. The Subjugation of Women. Cambridge, Mass: MIT Press, 1970 (1869).

NATIONAL GALLERY OF IRELAND. W.B. Yeats – A Centenary Exhibition 1868. Dublin: National Gallery, 1965.

NI EIREAMHON, Eibhlin. Two Great Irish Women, Maude Gonne MacBride and Countess Markievicz. Dublin: Fallon, 1971.

NI DHUBHGHAILL, C. Maire. Women in Ancient and Modern Ireland. Dublin: Kenny Press, 1971.

NULTY, Christina (ed). Images of Irish Women. Dublin: Crane Bag, Vol. 4 1980.

O'CONNELL, T.J. 100 Years of Progress: The Story of the Irish National Teachers' Organisation 1868–1968, Dublin: INTO, 1970's.

OWENS, Rosemary. Votes for Women: Irishwomen's Campaign for the Vote 1876–1915. (unpublished thesis). Dublin: Dept of History UCD, 1977.

OWENS BLACKBURNE, Elizabeth. Illustrious Irish Women. London: Tinsley, 1887.

PANKHURST, Emeline. My Own Story. London: 1914.

PLUNKETT, Pilkington and Russell. The United Irishwomen: Their Place, Work and Ideals. Dublin: Mansell, 1911.

ROSE, Catherine. The Female Experience: The Story of the Woman Movement in Ireland. Dublin: Arlen House, 1975.

SAYERS, Peig. An Old Woman's Reflections (trans. by, Seamus Ennis). London: OUP, 1962.

SHEEHY SKEFFINGTON, Andree D and Rosemary Owens (ed). Votes for Women: Irish Women's Struggle for the Vote. (pamphlet) Dublin: Skeffington and Owens, 1975.

SOMERFIELD, Henry. That Myriad Minded Man: A Biography of GW Russell (AE). Bucks: Colin Smythe, 1975.

SKINNIDER, Margaret. Doing My Bit for Ireland. New York: Century, 1917.

TOMLIN, Claire. The Life and Death of Mary Wollstonecraft. Middlesex: Penguin, 1977.

THOMPSON, William and Anna Wheeler. Appeal of One Half of the Human Race, Women, Against the Pretensions of the Other Half, Men, to Retain Them in Political, and Thence in Civil and Domestic Slavery (with a new Critical Introduction by Joseph Lee). Cork: C.P. Hyland, 1975 (1825).

VAN VORIS, Jacqueline. The Story of Constance de Markievicz and Her Fight for the Liberation of Ireland and Women. New York: The Feminist Press, 1972.

WARD, Margaret. Suffrage First Above All Else: An Account of the Irish Suffrage Movement. (Feminist Review No. 10) London: Pluto Press, 1982.

WARD, Margaret. Unmanageable Revolutionaries; Women and Irish Nationalists Kerry: Brandon, 1983.

WEBB, Irish Biography. Dublin: Gill, 1878.

WOLLSTONECRAFT, Mary. Vindication of the Rights of Women. Middlesex: Penguin, 1974 (1872).

COLLECTIONS

In National Library of Ireland: Irish Citizen (weekly Newspaper, ceased publication in 1920); Maire Comerford collection; Anna Parnell, the Tale of a Great Sham and Assorted Letters; Hanna Skeehy Skeffington Unsorted Papers; Suffrage Papers of 1975 Exhibition. Mary Hayden's papers.

In Public Records Office, Dublin: Irish Women Workers Union (IWWU), Minutes 1913 to 1960.

Archives Dept. UCD.

SUBJECT INDEX

Abbey Theatre 7, 8, 26, 44, 45
Adult Education College (ICA) 16, 37
Albert Hall, London 14
Alexandra College 19, 28, 32, 39, 43, 50, 54
America 8, 14, 17, 23, 27, 28, 33, 35, 38, 42, 45, 49, 51, 52
Anti Partition League 14,
Archbishop of Dublin 7, 55
Associated Countrywomen of the World (ACWW) 20
Bean na hEireann 20, 44
Bedford College, London 43
Belfast and District Trades Union Council 53
Boston Pilot 49
Brennan, John (see Sidney Gifford) 23
ni Bruadar, Gobait (see Albinia Broderick) 11
Camogie Association 24, 48
Central Remedial Clinic (CRC) 48
Church of Ireland Representative Body 19
CIE, Dublin 30
Citizen's Advice Bureau 53
Civil War (1922) 14, 15, 20, 33, 34, 39, 41, 42, 46, 54
Clones Lace 27
College of Surgeons 26, 53
Communist Party 18, 53
Conditions of Employment Bill (1935) 57
Connolly, James 12, 15, 22, 33, 42, 44, 53
Consultant Commissioner 11
Co-operative Movement 56
Cork Examiner 16
Croke Gaelic Club 24
Cuala Press 24
Cubism 30, 32
Cumann na mBan 11, 12, 13, 15, 22, 25, 46, 53, 57
Cumann na nGaedheal (1903) 40
Dail Eireann 13, 15, 28, 38, 41, 52
Dublin Weekly Freeman 34
Dublin Women's Suffrage Association 27
Embalmer 29
Englishwomen's Review 9
Eton College 30
Famine 8, 27
Fanagans Undertakers 29
Farmers Association Wexford 36
Feis Atha Cliath Shield 14
Feis Ceoil 50
Fenian 43, 49, 56, 57
Fianna Fail 13, 34, 41
Fodhla Printing Company 47
Folk Singer 41
Fox, RM 38

Friends of the National Collections of Ireland 50
Furey Brothers 21
Gaelic League 15, 17, 28, 31, 41, 43, 48
Gaiety Theatre 31
Gate Theatre 31, 37
Great Blasket Island 52
Guggenheim Fellowship 51
Hall, Mrs SC (see Anna Marie Fielding) 19
Hamman Hotel 34
Harpist 45
Hebrew 30
Holloway Jail 25
Home Rule 17, 55
Horse Show, Dublin 31, 36
India 16, 29
Inghinidhe na hEireann 20, 23, 25, 40, 42, 44, 57
Irish Academy of Letters 37, 47, 54
Irish Bulletin 46
Irish Citizen 9, 52
Irish Citizen Army 20, 26, 38, 42, 44
Irish College, Cloghaneely 48
Irish Congress of Trades Unions (ICTU) 9, 12, 22, 44
Irish Countrywoman 16
Irish Countrywomen's Association (ICA) 16, 20, 36, 37, 44
Irish Exhibition of Living Art 32
Irish Folklore Commission 52
Irish Freedom 11
Irish Homestead 44
Irish Literary Society London 31
Irishman 49
Irish Messenger 15
Irish Monthly 21
Irish National Theatre Society 26
Irish Nurses Organisation (INO) 54
Irish Pavilion Glasgow 32
Irish People 49
Irish Poor Clares 17
Irish Press 14
Irish Republican Army (IRA) 18
Irish Sisters of Charity 7
Irish Statesman 44
Irish Text Society (1899) 31
Irish Times 13
Irish Women Workers' Union (IWWU) 9, 12, 35, 44, 47
Irish Women's Franchise League 16, 52
Irish Women's Reform League 9
Irish Women's Suffrage Federation (1910) 9, 12
Irish Workers' Dramatic Company 35
Irish Workers' Textile Union Belfast 33
Islander 52
ITGWU 12, 15, 22, 26, 35

Jacobs Factory 26
Kilmainham Jail 12, 24, 26, 47
Labour Party 12, 15, 33
Ladies Land League 17, 49, 56, 57
Lancashire Mill Girls 25
Landsfeldt, Countess (see Eliza Gilbert) 23
Laundry Workers' Strike (1935) 9
League of Health and Beauty 48
Legion of Mary 51
Librarian 19, 30, 56
Little Sisters of St. Francis 34
Liverpool Repertory Company 7
Lock Out (1913) 18, 33, 35
London Palladium 14
Lord Mayor, Dublin 13
Loretto University College 40
Madame Steevens Hospital Dublin 21
Markswoman 53
Mater Hospital 29
Maxwell Brewer Academy of Irish Dancing 14
Medical Missionaries of Mary (MMM) 42
Middleton, Earl of 11
Midwife 10
Millworkers 33
Mines 23, 33
Missionaries 29, 34, 42, 51
Mna na Pobhlachta 11
Montez, Lola (see Eliza Gilbert) 23
Moran's Hotel 54
Mountjoy Jail 34
Municipal Gallery of Modern Art 32, 50
The Nation 11, 35, 46, 49
National BCG Committee 55
National Land League 17, 46, 49, 56
National Society for Women's Suffrage 9
National University of Ireland (NUI) 22, 28
Nightingale, Florence 19, 34
Northern Ireland Civil Rights Association 53
Nun of Kenmare (see Margaret Anna Cusack) 17
Olive Leaf Circle 27
Opera 28
Others and Broom 51
Pall Mall Gazette 46
Parliament of Women, London (1909) 16
Poor Clare Order 51
Primary School Teachers' Association 53
Printer 47
Proclamation 26
Producer 45
Rathmines & Rathgar Musical Society (R&R) 45

Red Cross 34
Republican Congress 30
Revolutionary Workers' Group (CPI) 53
Rising (1803) 18
Rising (1916) 12, 14, 15, 20, 22, 26, 34, 38, 41, 42, 44, 46, 47, 52, 53, 54, 55, 57
Royal Dublin Society (RDS) 20
Royal Irish Academy of Music 50
Royal University of Ireland 28, 32, 40, 52
Rural Organiser 20, 27, 36, 37
Rushwork 37
St. Ita's School 22, 41
St. Mary's Dominican Academy 48
St. Ultan's Hospital 20, 38, 55
St. Vincent's Hospital 7
Sacco and Vanzetti 51
Seanad 13, 15, 28, 48, 55, 57
Shan Van Vocht 11, 43
Shelbourne Hotel 53
Sinn Fein 11, 12, 14, 20, 23, 38, 40, 41, 42, 43, 49, 52, 57
Sisters of Mercy 39
Society of Prevention of Cruelty to Animals 31
Sportswoman 24
Spring Show Dublin 36
Stained Glass 30, 50
Story Teller 21, 52
Superstition, Victim of 13
Tailteann Silver Medal 24, 38
Textile Operatives' Society 22
Thompson, William 56
Traveller 21
Treaty (1921) 15, 18, 22, 25, 38, 41, 42, 43, 46, 52, 55, 57
Trinity College Dublin (TCD) 12, 19, 30, 43, 55
Truck Act 22
Ulster Anti Partition Council 43
Uncle Remus (see Rose Kavanagh) 34
United Ireland 11, 43, 46, 49
United Irishman 18
United Irishwomen (ICA) 36, 44
University College Cork (UCC) 16
University College Dublin (UCD) 22, 28, 30, 40, 50
William Roberts Prizeman in Classics 30
Witch 13, 19
Women's Franchise Movement 38
Women's International League for Peace & Freedom 33
Women's Prisoners' Defence League 25
Women's Social & Progressive League 52
The Workers' Dreadnought 38

Spinning Mills, Belfast